CONTENTS

FOREWORD AND ACKNOWLEDGEMENTS

In Ireland, two Acts have commonly been hailed as the New Consumer Charter. These are the Consumer Information Act, 1978, and the Sale of Goods and Supply of Services Act, 1980. This book outlines the statutory position in the main areas -Sale of Goods, Hire-Purchase, Guarantees and Consumer Information - affected by that legislation. Illustrative case law is also referred to.

The book is intended only as a guide. When dealing with an individual problem, one must expect to refer to the original sources, since there is no perfect substitute for a reading of the relevant legislation and the case law that is directly on point. Secondary sources - even where their scope is less modest than that of this book - often omit details of the law that can have an important bearing on one's legal position.

The introduction in 1991 of a Small Claims Procedure is of special relevance in Consumer Law, although that development is essentially a procedural one.

Of considerable significance also is E.C. Directive 93/13/EEC, now implemented in Ireland by S.I. No. 27 of 1995. The Directive and the implementing Regulations are primarily designed to eliminate unfair terms from consumer contracts. In broad terms, their net effect is to render any such term a nullity.

I take this opportunity to thank those who helped in the completion of this work, in particular D.J. Murphy and M. F. O'Byrne of Copy Design Bureau, Glasheen Road, Cork.

Denis Linehan
January,1996

TABLE OF CONTENTS

Sale of Goods

The consumer is....the king.

Paul Samuelson

CHAPTER 1 : SALE OF GOODS

The sale of goods transaction is governed principally by the Sale of Goods Act 1893, by the Sale of Goods and the Supply of Services Act, 1980, and also by the common law rules applicable to contracts generally. The 1893 Act, which was passed during what has been termed *the era of commercial codification,* was a consolidating measure. In the words of its drafter, Sir McKenzie Chalmers, — *"It endeavoured to produce as exactly as possible the existing law".* The Sale of Goods and the Supply of Services Act, the operative date for which is January 1, 1981, is an updating measure. Because of the high quality of the drafting of the legislation on sale of goods, the case-law on the transaction is mainly illustrative of the statutory principles.

Apart from the legislation already mentioned, there is a wide range of legislation which impacts peripherally on the sale of goods transaction. Thus, there is regulation of such matters as advertising, weights and measures, prices and taxation.

One is apt to think of the sale of goods transaction in the retail context. It should, however, be borne in mind that a high percentage of sales occur in the commercial rather than in the consumer setting, as goods pass along the chain of distribution - from manufacturer to exporter, to importer, to wholesaler, to retailer, and finally to the consumer.

FORMATION AND INTERPRETATION OF CONTRACTS OF SALE

General

Such matters as capacity to contract, the formalities of sale and time clauses in contracts of sale are referred to in Sections 1—10 of the Sale of Goods Act.

Definitions, Formalities and other Preliminary Matters

A contract of sale of goods is "... *a contract whereby the sellers transfers or agrees to transfer the property in goods for a money consideration called the price". Section 1(1).* See, e.g., *Flynn v Mackin and Mahon* (1974) I.R.101. A contract of sale may be either a sale or an agreement to sell. A sale comprises both a contract and a conveyance, so that the property in the goods sold passes to the buyer when the contract is made. An agreement to sell is a contract only, and does not result in the immediate passing of the property in the goods sold to the buyer. The importance of the distinction between a sale and an agreement to sell lies in its effect on the timing' of the passing of the property in goods sold between seller and buyer. The time when the property passes is, in turn, important in relation to:— (a). the loss or destruction of the goods, (b). the buyer's remedies against a defaulting seller, and (c). a seller's remedies against a defaulting buyer. See, e.g., *Clarke v Reilly & Sons* 96 I.L.T.R. 96.

The principles which govern capacity to conclude contracts of sale are coextensive with the general principles governing capacity to contract. *Section 2.*

Formalities are prescribed for contracts of sale. *Section 3 and 4.* Where the price involved exceeds £10, a contract of sale will be unenforceable unless made in accordance with the following formalities:-

a. *The buyer must accept and receive part of the goods sold; or*

b. *The buyer must give something to bind the contract; or*

c. *A written memorandum of the contract, signed by the party of his agent to be charged, must be made.*

Kirwan v Price, (1958) Ir. Jur. Rep. 56
The plaintiff here agreed to purchase the defendant's horse, subject to the horse being passed by a veterinary surgeon. When the examination was successfully completed, the plaintiff tendered payment, but the defendant refused to accept it. The plaintiff's claim for specific performance failed. The contract fell within the provisions of Section 4 of the Act, and the requirement of a written note or memorandum had not been fulfilled.

The Act recognises four categories of goods. *Section 5*. These are: − existing goods, future goods, specific goods and unascertained goods. The class of goods involved in a particular contract may be of importance in determining whether the contract will operate as a sale or as an agreement to sell.

A contract for the sale of specific goods which have perished without the knowledge of the seller is void. *Section 6*. If specific goods, which are comprised in an agreement to sell, perish before the property in them passes to the buyer, the contract is avoided provided the seller was not at fault. *Section 7*.

The price in a contract of sale may be:-

a. Fixed in the contract;

b. Fixed in accordance with the contract;

c. ·Determined by a course of dealing between , the parties; or

d. Where none of the foregoing applies, will be a reasonable price. *Section 8 and 9*.

Time clauses are not of the essence in contracts of sale, unless the circumstances show a contrary intention. Section 10. One must, however, normally imply a term that the obligations of the parties will be satisfied within a reasonable time.

CONDITIONS AND WARRANTIES

Terms Generally

Terms in a contract of sale may be express or implied. Parties are in general free to make their own express contracts, and many businesses insist on using their own standard conditions of sale. Certain terms are, however, implied on the buyer's behalf in every contract of sale by virtue of the provisions noted below.

Certain of the implied terms are conditions, and others are warranties. This distinction is important in the determination of the remedies available to a buyer where an implied term has been broken.

The terms to be considered establish a basis for the contractual liability of a seller. It should be remembered however that, on the sale of a defective product, a seller may also be liable for the tort of negligence. See, e.g., *Donoghue v. Stevenson* (1932) A.C. 562. Moreover, even without proof of negligence, under the terms of the Liability for Defective Products Act, 1991, a producer may be held liable in tort for damage caused by a defect in his product.

Terms Implied by Statute

Where a contract of sale is not severable, and the buyer has accepted the goods, or part thereof, the breach of any condition to be fulfilled by the seller can only be treated as a breach of warranty, and not as a ground for rejecting the goods and treating the contract as repudiated. *Section 11, S.G.A., 1893*, as inserted by Section 10, S.G.S.S.A, 1980. This provision, which applies in the absence of a term to the contrary, alters the general rule of contract that the breach of a condition entitles a party to repudiation: it extends to all terms, whether express or implied.

The implied terms will now be considered. First, in general there is an implied condition that the seller has a right to sell the goods, an implied warranty that the goods are free from encumbrances and an implied warranty that the buyer should enjoy quiet possession. *Section 12, S.G.A., 1893*, as insered by Section 10, S.G.S.S.A., 1980. See, e.g., *United Dominians Trust (Ire.) Ltd. v. Shannon Caravans Ltd.* (1976) I.R.225. These terms are not, however, implied in a contract where it appears from the circumstances that the seller should transfer only such title as he may have. In the latter situation, however, there are implied warranties that the seller has disclosed all encumbrances known to him, and also that neither he nor any third party who is privy with him will disturb the buyer's quiet possession to the extent to which title has been transferred.

Secondly, in a sale by description, there is an implied condition that the goods will correspond with the description. If a sale by description should also be a sale by sample, it is not sufficient that the bulk of the goods corresponds with the sample if the goods do not also correspond with the description. *Section 13,* S.G.A., 1893, as inserted by Section 10, S.G.S.S.A., 1980.

Thirdly, where a seller sells goods in the course of a business, there is an implied condition that the goods supplied are of merchantable quality, except that there is no such condition:- *"(a). As regards defects specifically drawn to the buyer's attention before the contract is made, or (b). If the buyer examines the goods before the contract is made, as regards defects which that examination ought to have revealed". Section 14 (2),* S.G.A., 1893, as inserted by Section 10, S.G.S.S.A., 1980.

The concept of merchantable quality is elaborated on in the new Section 14 (3) as follows:-

"Goods are of merchantable quality if they are as fit for the purpose or purposes for which goods of that kind are commonly bought and as durable as it is reasonable to expect having regard to any description applied to them, the price (if relevant) and all the other relevant circumstances, and any reference in this Act to unmerchantable goods shall be construed accordingly".

Egan v. McSweeney (1956) 90 I.L.T.R. 40.

The defendant was a coal merchant with whom the plaintiff had a course of dealing lasting some twenty years. The plaintiff ordered two bags of coal and, when this was ignited, an explosion occurred and the plaintiff was seriously injured.

Although he had not been negligent, the defendant was held liable under Section 14 (2) of the 1893 Act. The coal had been supplied by a person who dealt in coal, and a condition that the coal was of merchantable quality was therefore implied. This term had been broken, and the plaintiff recovered damages for the breach.

Fourthly, a condition that goods sold are reasonably fit for a particular purpose is also implied in certain circumstances, as follows:- *"Where the seller sells goods in the course of a business and the buyer, expressly or by implication makes known to the seller any particular purpose for which the goods are being bought, there is an implied condition that the goods supplied are reasonably fit for that purpose, whether or not that is a purpose for which such goods are commonly supplied expect where the circumstances show that the buyer does not rely, or that it is unreasonable for him to rely, on the seller's skill or judgment".* Section 14 (4), S.G.A., 1893, as inserted by Section 10, S.G.S.S.A., 1980. See, e.g., Draper *v. Rubenstein,* 59 I.L.T.R. 119.

Fifthly, a number of conditions are implied in relation to sales by sample. The bulk must correspond with the sample and, also, the buyer must be allowed a reasonable opportunity of comparing the bulk with the sample. In addition, a condition is implied whereby the bulk must be free from any defect that would make it unmerchantable, which defect would not be apparent on a reasonable examination of the sample. *Section 15, S.G.A., 1893, as inserted by Section 10, S.G.S.S.A., 1980.*

A sale by sample is defined as follows:-

"A contract of sale is a contract for sale by sample where there is a term in the contract, express or implied, to that effect".

Sixthly, in a contract for the sale of goods, there are implied warranties that spare parts and an adequate aftersale service will be made available by the seller in such circumstances as are stated in an offer, description or advertisement by the seller on behalf of the manufacturer or on his own behalf. The warranties last for the period stated or, if none is stated, for a reasonable period. *Section 12,* S.G.S.S.A.

Seventhly, in every contract for the sale of a motor vehicle (except a contract in which the buyer is a person whose business it is to deal in motor vehicles), there is an implied condition that at the time of delivery of the vehicle under the contract it is free from any defect which would render it a danger to the public, including persons travelling in the vehicle. *Section 13,* S.G.S.S.A. This condition, which is implied without prejudice to any other condition or warranty, does not apply where:—

"a. it is agreed between the seller and the buyer that the vehicle is not intended for use in the condition in which it is to be delivered to the buyer under the contract; and

19

b. *a document consisting of a statement to that effect is signed by or on behalf of the seller and the buyer and given to the buyer prior to or at the time of such delivery, and*

c. *it is shown that the agreement referred to in paragraph (a). is fair and reasonable."*

An eighth and final implied term pertains to the liability of finance houses. Where goods are sold to a buyer dealing as consumer and, in relation to the sale, an agreement is entered into by the buyer with another person acting in the course of a business (in this section referred to as a finance house) for the repayment to the finance house of money paid by the finance house to the seller in respect of the price of the goods, the finance house shall be deemed to be a party to the sale. In this situation, the finance house and the seller shall, jointly and severally, be answerable to the buyer for breach of the contract of sale and for any misrepresentations made by the seller with respect to the goods. *Section 14,* S.G.S.S.A.

Exclusion of the Terms implied by Statute

Exclusion of the terms implied by statute in contracts of sale is now regulated by Section 11, S.G.S.S.A. This provision affects the terms regarding title, correspondence with description, merchantable quality, fitness for purpose and correspondence with sample.

It is an offence for a person in the course of a business to issue any written statement to the effect that any of these implied terms is restricted or excluded otherwise than under Section 55 of the S.G.A., 1893. The statement referred to may be by notice, advertisement, label or by any other document.

Section 55 (which has been introduced in a new form by Section 22, S.G.S.S.A.) provides that any term in a contract purporting to exempt the seller from the implied obligations on title shall be void. It also provides that any term purporting to exempt the seller from the implied terms as to correspondence with description, merchantable quality, fitness for purpose or correspondence with sample shall be void where the buyer *deals as consumer* and shall, in any other case, not be enforceable except to such extent as it is shown to be fair and reasonable.

The concept of *dealing as consumer* is elaborated on in Section 3, S.G.S.S.A., as follows:-

" .... *a party to a contract is said to deal as consumer in relation to another party if:—*

a.   *he neither makes the contract in the course of a business, nor holds himself out as doing so, and*

b.   *the other party does make the contract in the course of a business, and*

c.   *the goods or services supplied under or in pursuance of the contract are of a type ordinarily supplied for private use or consumption.*

(2). On :—

a.   a sale by competitive tender, or

b.   a sale by auction:—

> *(i) of goods of a type, or*
> *(ii) by or on behalf of a person of a class*
> *defined by the Minister by order,*
the buyer is not in any circumstances to be regarded as dealing as consumer.

(3). Subject to this, it is for those claiming that a party does not deal as consumer to show that he does not".

The principle introduced by the substituted Section 55 is new. Previously, the implied terms in question — with the exception of the term regarding title — could be excluded by appropriate clauses.

TRANSFER OR PROPERTY BETWEEN SELLER AND BUYER

Meaning of Property

The term property as used in Sections 16-20 is, for most practical purposes, synonymous with ownership. These Sections establish three main propositions. First, no property in goods can pass until the goods are ascertained. Secondly, the time when the property in ascertained goods passes is governed by the intention of the parties. And, thirdly, the risk of the loss to goods prima facie passes with the property.

Transfer of Property, and the Risk Factor

Subject to the qualification that the property in goods cannot pass until the goods are ascertained, the general rule is that the property passes when the parties intend it to pass. Sections 16 and 17.

Clarke v. Reilly 96 I.L.T.R. 96.

The plaintiff here contracted with the defendants for the supply of a new car. Payment consisted of a trade-in, and a cheque for the balance of the purchase price. Pending delivery of the new car, the plaintiff obtained permission to use his old car and, while using it, was involved in an accident. He succeeded in an action for specific performance. Although the defendants had not cashed the cheque, the grant of permission to the plaintiff to use his old car was an indication that both parties had intended the property in the car to pass on making the contract.

A number of rebuttable presumptions are specified to assist in ascertaining the intention of the parties. *Section 18.* Moreover, it is provided that the property in goods cannot pass while the seller reserves a right of disposal. *Section 19.*

The general rule is that the risk of loss or damage to goods follows the property. *Section 20.* There are two exceptions to this rule. First, where one party causes a delay in the delivery of goods, that party is responsible for any loss arising out of the delay, irrespective of which party has the property in the goods. Secondly, where one party occupies a special position with respect to goods, that party is responsible for any loss arising to the goods by virtue of a breach of a duty incidental to the special position, irrespective of which party has the property in the goods.

TRANSFER OF TITLE TO GOODS

Nemo Dat Quod Non Habet

The general rule is that a person can convey only the title which he has – *nemo dat quod non habet.* The law thus protects ownership. There are exceptions to the general rule: most of these exceptions may be seen as protecting the market place rather than ownership.

The foregoing rule and exceptions are covered in Section 21-26, S.G.A.

Exceptions

There are a number of exceptions to the general rule that no person can give a better title to goods than the one which he has. First, a party who is selling as agent can confer the title which the principal has. *Section 21(1).* An agent can be regarded as the alter ego of the principal.

Secondly, a factor who has a defective title can give a good title to a third party who buys in the ordinary course of business, and who takes the goods in good faith and without notice of the defect in the factor's title. *Section 21(1) (D).* A factor can be defined as a general mercantile agent who deals with a specified category or categories of goods. Examples are car dealers and furniture auctioneers.

Thirdly, a party with no title, or with only a defective title, can give a good title to a party who takes for value and in good faith, provided the true owner is estopped from denying the validity of the transaction. *Section 21(2) (a).* The basis of this exception may be described as follows:- *Whenever the true owner of goods invests another with the indicia of property to them, this operates as a representation to innocent third parties that the person entrusted with the indicia of property can deal with the goods as owner. The true owner cannot seek to refute this representation against a person who buys the goods in good faith and without notice of the defective title.* See, e.g., *Henderson & Co. v. Williams* (1895) 1 Q.B. 521.

Fourthly, a party who lacks title can confer a good title provided the sale is under a special power or under a court order. *Section 21(2) (B).* For example, a sheriff can give a good title when selling under an execution order.

Fifthly, a party without title can confer a good title by a sale in market overt, provided the buyer takes in good faith and for value. *Section 22.* See, e.g., Bishopsgate *Motor Finance Corporation Ltd. v. Transport Brakes Ltd.* (1949) 1 K.B. 322. A market overt – which can be established by charter, custom or statute – is one which is *"open, public and legally constituted". Per Jervis J., in Lee v. Bayes* (1856) 18 C.B. 599 at 601.

Sixthly, a party with a voidable title may give a good title to a third party who takes for value and without notice of the defect, provided the transaction occurs before the voidable title is avoided. *Section 23.*

Anderson v. Ryan (1967) I.R. 34.

The owner of a Mini motor car exchanged it for a car which, unknown to him, had been stolen. The Mini was subsequently sold to the defendant, who bought it in good faith and for value. The defendant, in turn, sold the Mini to the plaintiff. A few days later, the police repossessed the car from the plaintiff, who sued for the cost of the car. A judgment in his favour was over-turned on appeal. In applying Section 23, the court held that the defendant had acquired a good title to the car, because the original owner of it had not avoided the defective title before the defendant had completed the purchase.

Seventhly, a seller in possession of goods, which he has already sold in a previous transaction, may give a good title to a third party who takes in good faith and without notice of the previous sale. *Section 25(1)*.

Eightly, a buyer in possession of goods, in respect of which the seller has a lien or other right, may give a good title to a third party who takes in good faith and without notice of the right of the original seller. *Section 25(2)*. See, e.g., *Re Interview Ltd*. (1975) I.R. 382.

The effect of a writ of execution on a sale of goods is covered in Section 26. This provides that a writ of execution shall bind the property in goods subject to it as from the time when the writ is delivered to the sheriff for execution. Even after such delivery, a person who buys the goods for value and in good faith acquires a valid title.

PERFORMANCE OF THE CONTRACT OF SALE

Open and Formal Contracts Contrasted
A seller's basic obligations under a contract of sale are to transfer title and to deliver conforming goods to the buyer. The basic obligations of the buyer, on the other hand, are to accept the goods and to pay the price in accordance with the contract.

Some contracts of sale will specify the particulars of performance - in particular, many trading concerns insist on their own standard conditions of sale.

Other contracts of sale, however, are *open*. The issues that may arise on the performance of the latter type of contract include the following:- the proper time, place and manner for delivery; the responsibility for insuring the goods during carriage; the proper time, place and manner for payment; and the extent of the buyer's rights of inspection and rejection. The number of issues that could arise on performance is indeed myriad.

The statutory provisions on performance do not anticipate every conceivable controversy that may occur in the course of a sale. They treat only a number of selective issues, and provide for their resolution where this has not been done expressly by the parties.

Statutory Provisions

The delivery of goods and the payment of the price must be in accordance with the contract. *Section 27.* See, e.g., *Industria Tessile Ambrosiana Marra C.S.P.A. v Hydrotyte Limited,* (H.Ct., 9/7/1974). Delivery of the goods and payment of the price are presumed to be concurrent conditions unless the contrary is specified. *Section 28.* See, e.g., *Macauley & Cullen v. Horgan* (1925) I.R. 1.

General rules are set out in Section 29 governing the proper method, time and place for delivery of goods where the contract is not specific on these matters. 'The buyer's position where the goods delivered are incorrect either as to quantity or description is contained in Section 30.

A seller may not deliver by instalments in the absence of a prior agreement. *Section 31.* Moreover, whether or not a deviation from the terms of an instalment contract amounts to a repudiation of the contract is a question of fact in any given case.

Delivery to a carrier by a seller is, prima facie, delivery to the buyer. *Section 32.*

Michel Freres Societe Anonyme v. Kilkenny Woollen Mills Ltd. (1961) I.R. 157.
The plaintiff, a French manufacturing firm, contracted with the defendants for the delivery of a consignment of yarn. A date for delivery - but not a place of delivery - was specified. The plaintiffs consigned the goods to a carrier before the agreed date, but the goods did not reach the defendant's premises until two weeks after the date agreed. When the defendants rejected the goods for breach of the time clause, the plaintiffs sued for the price. The action failed. The facts showed that the carriage contract made the carrier an agent of the seller, and that the carrier was not to deliver until the price was paid. The court decided that the presumption raised by Section 32 had thus been rebutted.

A carriage contract arranged by a seller must, unless otherwise agreed with the buyer, conform to the general standard that it be reasonable. Where delivery of goods is to involve carriage by sea, a seller has a duty to notify the buyer of the necessity for insurance.

Where the seller takes the carriage risks in respect of goods to be delivered at a distant place, the buyer must nevertheless bear the risks of wear and tear incidental to carriage. *Section 33.* A buyer is not deemed to have accepted goods until he has been given a reasonable opportunity of examining them. *Section 34.* See, e.g., *Marry v. Merville Dairy* (1954) 88 I.L.T.R. 129.

A buyer is deemed to have accepted goods in three cases:- first, when he intimates an acceptance to the seller; secondly, when goods have been delivered to him, and he does any act in relation to them which is inconsistent with the ownership of the seller; and thirdly, where after the lapse of a reasonable time, a buyer retains goods without intimating a rejection of them to the seller. *Section 35.*

Although a buyer is not required to return goods which have properly been rejected, he must notify the seller of the rejection. *Section 36.*

A buyer is liable for a wrongful refusal to take delivery of goods in accordance with the contract. *Section 37.* The extent of his liability depends on whether or not his failure to take delivery amounts to a repudiation of the contract.

RIGHTS OF AN UNPAID SELLER AGAINST THE GOODS

Monetary and Proprietary Rights Contrasted

A seller may have two classes of remedy in the

event of a default by the buyer. First, he may have a monetary remedy - an action either for the price or for damages. Secondly, he may have rights in respect of the goods comprised in the sale; this second category of rights will now be considered.

Account of the Proprietary Rights

An unpaid seller is defined as one who has not been paid, in accordance with a contract, for goods sold. *Section 38.* An unpaid seller's statutory rights in rem against the goods sold are outlined in Sections 39-48. The rights given include a lien, stoppage in transit and resale; these rights are available regardless of who has the property in the goods. An unpaid seller is also given the right to *withhold delivery* of the goods, but only if he has retained the property in them. *Section 39(2).*

First, an unpaid seller can exercise a lien; the buyer's insolvency is not a prerequisite to this right. Where an unpaid seller has made part delivery of goods over which he is entitled to exercise a lien, the lien may be exercised over the undelivered goods, unless this right has been waived.

The right to a lien depends on the seller having possession, either actual or constructive, of the goods sold. Thus, the lien is lost if the buyer acquires possession of the goods. It is also lost if the seller waives the right. *Section 41-43.*

Secondly, an unpaid seller, who has lost possession of goods comprised in a contract, can *stop the goods in transit.* This right is dependent on the insolvency of the buyer.

It has been stated that,— *"The essential feature of a stoppage in transit is that the goods should be .... in the possession of a middle man".* Per Cairns., L.J., in Schotmans v Lancs. and Yorks Railway (1867) 2 Ch. App. 332 at 338. An unpaid seller can exercise the right to stop goods in either of two ways - he can take actual possession of the goods; alternatively, he can serve notice of assertion of the right to stoppage on the person who has actual possession. *Sections 44-46.*

Thirdly, although the original sale is not generally rescinded by the exercise of a lien or stoppage in transit, nevertheless, an unpaid seller has a *right to resell* in certain situations. *Section 48.* These are as follows:—

a. *The seller can resell, as owner, if the property in the goods has not passed to the original buyer;*

b. *The seller may resell if the original buyer has repudiated the contract, either expressly or impliedly;*

c. *The seller may resell if the original contract expressly provides for resale on the buyer's default;*

d. *The seller may resell if he has already exercised a lien or stoppage;*

e. The seller may resell where the goods are
    perishable, and where the buyer does not
    pay or tender the price within a reasonable
    time;

f. The seller may resell where he has given
    notice of his intention to do so to the
    buyer, and the latter does not pay or
    tender the price within a reasonable time.

Fourthly, as already noted, an unpaid seller may
withhold delivery of goods provided that the
property in them has not passed to the buyer.
Section 39(2). The distinction between this right
and the right to a lien is largely technical.

Finally, recent case law has established the
additional right in rem for an unpaid seller to
trace goods comprised in the contract. Cases in
point are:— *Re Interview Limited,* (1975) I.R.
382, and *Aluminium Industrie D.V. v Romalpa
Ltd.* (1976) I.W.L.R. 676.

Re Interview Ltd. (1975) I.R. 382.
*An Irish company, E.I.I., distributed goods
manufactured by the German Company, Tele-
funken, under an agreement whereby the
passing of property was subject to payment of
the price. By agreement, Interview Ltd., who
owned one third of E.I.I.'s share capital, took
over the distrubutership through a subsidiary.
The terms of the original agreement were
retained. E.I.I. transferred their stock-in-hand
to Interview Ltd., which subsequently went*

*into receivership. The German company succ-
essfully established the precedence of its right
to trace the ownership of the goods over the
rights of the receiver. Since Interview Ltd. did
not receive the goods in good faith and without
notice of the rights of the original sellers, the
right to trace remained.*

The above cases have established that an unpaid
seller has the right to trace goods which are in the
hands of the buyer, of a receiver, or of a liquidator.
An unpaid seller has, moreover, the right to the
proceeds of sale in respect of any of the goods
which have been sold. The right to trace can in
certain circumstances extend to any products
made from the goods sold. See, e.g., *Borden
(U.K.) v Scottish Timber Products* (1979) 3 All
E.R. 961.

ACTIONS FOR BREACH OF CONTRACT

General
The remedies of specific performance and
damages may be available to either party to a
contract of sale when the other party is in default.
The available remedy in any given case is
determined in accordance with the provisions
listed below.

The seller is entitled in certain circumstances
to recover the price from a defaulting buyer; this
is effectively the right to *specifically enforce* the
contract. In other circumstances, a seller will be
entitled only to the lesser remedy of damages for

breach of contract. It will be seen that a buyer likewise is sometimes entitled to a specific delivery of the goods bought and, at other times, is restricted to an action of damages.

Provision is also made for the assessment of damages when these constitute the appropriate remedy.

Actions for the Price, Damages and Possession

Where the price has not been paid in accordance with contract, a seller can sue for it where either: – (a). the property in the goods has passed to the buyer, or (b). the time for payment of the price was fixed without reference either to the time when the property in the goods should pass, or to the delivery date. *Section 49.* See, e.g., *Achates Investment Co. v. Cork Cooperative Marts Ltd.,* (1580-1975, H.Ct., Unrep., 15-12-1976). Where a buyer has not paid the price under a contract in circumstances other than those noted in (a) and (b) above, the seller can sue only for damages for non-acceptance. *Section 50.* The measure of damages is *".... the estimated loss directly and naturally resulting, in the ordinary course of events"* from the breach. *Section 50(2).* This measure is prima facie the difference between the market price and the contract price. *Section 50(3).*

A buyer can sue for damages if the seller fails to deliver in accordance with the contract. *Section 51.* The measure of general damages here is calculated in the same way as in an action by the seller. See, e.g., *Macauley & Cullen v. Horgan* (1952) I.R. 1. If a seller is in breach of a contract to deliver specific or ascertained goods, the buyer may — at the discretion of the court — be granted specific performance of the contract. *Section 52.* It has been said that:— *"The power vested in the courts to order the delivery of a particular chattel is discretionary and ought not to be exercised when the chattel is an ordinary article of commerce, and of no special value or interest and not alleged to be of any special value to the plaintiff, and where damages would fully compensate".* Per Swinfen Eady, *M.R., in Whiteley v Hilt* (1918) 2 K.B. 808 at 819.

In the event of a breach of warranty by the seller, or where the buyer elects or is compelled to treat the breach of a condition as a breach of warranty, the buyer may in the alternative:— (a). set up the breach of warranty in diminution or extinction of the price, or (b). maintain an action for damages for the breach of warranty. *Section 53.* There is a qualification to the foregoing:— namely, a buyer who is a consumer and who is not purchasing in the course of business - even when compelled to treat a breach of condition as a breach of warranty - will still have the power of rescission if the seller fails to remedy the breach.

It is provided that either party, where the other is in default, can where appropriate recover interest or special damages, or can recover money paid in the event of failure of consideration. *Section 54.* The rationale of special damages can be explained as follows:— *When a contract is made between parties who know of special circumstances to it, and who are aware that special loss will arise in the event of a breach, there is an implied liability to pay "special" damages if such a breach occurs.*

SUPPLEMENTARY PROVISIONS

General

The supplementary provisions of the Sale of Goods Act, 1893, cover, inter alia, the interpretation of the Acts, auction sales, definitions and international sales.

Interpretation, Auction Sales and other Supplementary Matters

Implied terms in contracts of sale can, in general be excluded by express provision. Section 55). There are exceptional cases. First, any attempt to exclude the implied terms as to title, freedom from encumbrances and quiet possession is void. Secondly, there are special provisions regarding the exclusion of implied terms as to correspondence with description, merchantable quality, reasonable fitness and correspondence of bulk with sample: any attempt to exclude these provisions shall be void where the buyer deals as consumer and shall, in any other case not be enforceable except to such extent as it is shown to be fair and reasonable.

The question of what is a *reasonable time* within the meaning of the legislation is a question of fact. *Section 56.*

A declaratory provision states that the rights, duties, etc., arising under the Act are enforceable by action. *Section 57.* There are special provisions on sales by auction. A seller or his agent may not bid at an auction unless prior notification of intent to do so has been given. Any sale contravening this rule may be treated as fraudulent by the buyer. Also, a sale by auction may be notified to be subject to a reserved price. *Section 58.*

All law applicable to contracts of sale, including case law, statute law and customary law, is preserved except in so far as it is inconsistent with the legislation. *Section 61.*

In an international contract of sale, the parties may dictate their own terms of contract without reference to the legislation. Unless however a contract of sale is truly international, the parties cannot seek to exclude the implied terms under Sections 12-15 of the 1893 Act, except to the extent already outlined.

Finally, it can be noted that the definition of *goods* within the legislation includes all chattels personal other than things in action and money. *Section 62.* The term includes emblements (industrial growing crops), and things attached to or forming part of the land which are agreed to be severed before sale or under the contract of sale. See, e.g., *Scully v. Corboy* (1950) I.R. 140.

Hire-Purchase

So far as my coin would stretch; and where it would not, I have used my credit.

Henry IV, Part I

CHAPTER II : HIRE-PURCHASE

The hire-purchase transaction is governed principally by the Hire Purchase Act 1946, the Hire Purchase (Amendment) Act 1960, the Sale of Goods and Supply of Services Act, 1980, and also by the common law rules applicable to contracts generally.

The credit society has brought about a dramatic increase in the use of hire-purchase, and of other credit transactions which are alternative to it. Such alternatives include leasing, conditional sale, credit sale, house credit and credit card transactions. The type of credit facilites made available by financial institutions and businesses at any time depends on a wide range of considerations. Relevant, for example, will be customer needs, taxation implications and the legal regulations of the different facilities.

Financial institutions play an important role in the provision of hire-purchase facilities. Approximately fifty per cent of the total of hire-purchase agreements are made between the hirer and a finance company, rather than between the hirer and a trader. As will be seen later, there are a number of forms which the *partnership* between financial institution and the trader can take.

HIRE-PURCHASE DEFINED

The components of hire-purchase are, first, a bailment and, secondly, an agreement or an option to purchase. Therefore, a person taking goods on hire-purchase becomes a bailee of the goods, and also acquires the right to obtain the property in the goods in accordance with the agreement.

The present form of hire-purchase is commonly ascribed to the implications of the decisions in two cases, namely, *Lee v Butler* (1893) 2 Q.B. 318, and *Helby v Matthews* (1895) A.C. 471.

Under Section 1, H.P.A., 1946, a hire-purchase agreement means:—

"An agreement for the bailment of goods under which the bailee may buy the goods or under which the property in the goods will or may pass to the bailee and where by virtue of two or more agreements, none of which by itself constitutes a hire-purchase agreement, there is a bailment of goods and either the bailee may buy the goods, or the property therein will or may pass to the bailee, the agreements shall be treated for the purpose of this Act as a single agreement made at the time when the last of the agreements was made."

TRANSACTIONS SIMILAR TO HIRE-PURCHASE

One type of transaction similar to hire-purchase is the *credit sale agreement*. This is defined as

"An agreement for the sale of goods under which the purchase price is payable by five or more instalments". Section 1, H.P.A., 1946. The property in goods subject to a credit sale agreement passes to the buyer as soon as the agreement is made, unless a contrary intention is expressed or implied. The Sale of Goods Act, 1893, as amended, applies to credit sales in the same way that it applies to other contracts of sale. Moreover, many provisions of the hire-purchase legislation also refer to credit sales.

Another credit transaction which resembles hire-purchase is the *conditional sale agreement.* This is one type of agreement to sell as defined in the Sale of Goods Act, 1893. The passing of the property in goods subject to such a transaction is conditional upon payment of the final instalment of the price. Conditional sales are governed by the Sale of Goods Act, 1893, as amended, and may, in certain circumstances, be governed by the hire-purchase legislation.

Finally, *hiring agreements* have some affinity with hire-purchase. Such agreements involve a bailment of hire, although the hirer acquires no option to purchase the goods.

Hiring agreements take a number of forms. One form is the operating lease, which is normally long term, and under which the lessor is responsible for repairs. Another form is the financial lease, which is also normally long term, and under which the lessor is not responsible for repairs. Thirdly, there is the rental agreement - used for example in relation to televisions; these agreements are normally short term, and under them the lessor usually accepts responsibility for repairs.

Agreements whereby goods are let on hire to a person *dealing as a consumer* now import implied terms on such matters as merchantable quality and fitness for purpose which are similar to the terms implied in hire-purchase agreements. *Section 38,* S.G.S.S.A., 1980.

FORMALITIES OF HIRE-PURCHASE AGREEMENTS

The hire-purchase legislation prescribes formalities designed to inform persons of the terms of their hire-purchase agreements. These formalities also have an evidentiary purpose; the requirement of a written record minimises the possibility of future dispute as to the terms of an agreement.

Certain information must be given to a hirer before and after an agreement is concluded, and this information must be given in the manner specified. Failure to comply with the formalities will, in general, render an agreement unenforceable.

The formalities will now be considered. First, before a hire-purchase agreement is concluded, the owner must state in writing the cash price to a prospective hirer, otherwise than in the note or memorandum of the agreement. This requirement will be deemed to be complied with if either:—

a. The hirer has inspected the goods prior to entering the contract, and at the time of inspection a ticket or label was attached to the goods clearly stating the cash price; or

b. The hirer selected the goods from a catalogue, price list or advertisement, which clearly set out the case price. Section 31(1)(a) and (b), H.P.A., 1946.

Secondly, every hire-purchase agreement must be in writing and signed by all parties. The writing (the note or memorandum) must contain:—

a. A statement of the hire-purchase price and of the cash price;

b. Particulars (dates and amounts) of the instalments to be paid;

c. A list of the goods comprised in the agreement; and

d. A notice in the form set out in the schedule to the 1946 Act, setting out the hirer's right to terminate the agreement and also the restriction on the owner's right to recover the goods. Section 3(2), H.P.A. 1946, as amended by Section 23, H.P.A.A., 1960.

The note or memorandum will satisfy the legislation only if signed after all the prescribed information is inserted. See, e.g., *Mercantile Credit Company of Ireland Ltd. v. Cahill* 98 I.L.T.R. 79; and *The British Wagon Credit Company v. Hennebry* 97 I.L.T.R. 123.

A hire-purchase agreement which does not comply with either of the foregoing formalities is generally unenforceable against either the hirer or any guarantor. A court may make an order enforcing an agreement, notwithstanding the absence of the second formality discussed above, if to do so is considered *just and equitable* in the circumstances. This discretion is not exercised lightly.

United Dominions Trust Ltd. v. Nestor (1962) I.R. 140.
The plaintiff and the defendant in this case had entered into a binding hire-purchase agreement for three articles of agricultural equipment. This was altered by a subsequent parol agreement, which the defendant breached. In the ensueing litigation, the judge adjudged non-compliance with the statutory provisions to be fatal to the plaintiffs' claim and stated:— "I wish to bring home to hire purchase companies the adviseability of a strict compliance with the statutory provisions. I make this comment because I regret to say that it has been my experience that insufficient care is taken in many cases in the making and signing of these agreements".

Thirdly, a copy of the note or memorandum must be sent to the hirer within fourteen days of the making of the agreement. Non-compliance has the same consequences as in relation to the second formality discussed. Section 3(2)(d) H.P.A. 1946, as amended by section 21 H.P.A.A. 1960.

Fourthly, the owner must supply, at the hirer's request, a copy of the note or memorandum of the agreement, and a statement signed by the owner giving an account of the state of the instalments. Section 7 H.P.A., 1946, as amended by Section 24 H.P.A.A. 1960.

RESTRICTION ON REPOSSESSION BY THE OWNER

The owner's right to repossess hired goods, unfettered in the early stages of the development of hire-purchase, was open to abuse. It could be exercised in a *snatch back,* upon a slight default by a hirer, after a considerable number of instalments had been paid. Whereas the owner could thus increase his profit by redisposing of the goods, the hirer would have lost his option to purchase.

Snatch back malpractices were undermined by the hire-purchase legislation. Sections 12-17, 1946 Act, and Section 25, 1960 Act. Now, where one-third of the hire-purchase price has been paid or tendered, the owner is precluded from enforcing any right to repossess the hired goods otherwise than by court action. The court, in any such action, has wide powers. For example, it may order specific delivery of the goods to the owner (without giving the hirer an option to pay their value); alternatively, it may order the transfer to the hirer of the owner's title to a part of the goods and the specific delivery of the remainder to the owner.

The protection afforded the hirer by Section 12 was referred to by Murnaghan J. in *United Dominions Trust Ltd. v. Byrne* (1955) I.R. 77 at 81:— *"This section seems to me to contain one of the fundamental restrictions imposed by the Legislature on hire-purchase transactions, and stipulates in the circumstances mentioned in the section that an owner of goods let under a hire-purchase agreement cannot recover possession of such goods otherwise than by action".*

TRANSFER OF PROPERTY AND THIRD PARTY RIGHTS

A hirer under a hire-purchase agreement is merely a contractual bailee of the goods comprised in the agreement. Pending the exercise of the right to purchase, the hirer has only a special property in the goods which is less than ownership. A hirer, under general principles of bailment, may use and dispose of the goods hired only in accordance with the objectives of the bailment. Moreover, hire-purchase agreements almost invariably restrict a hirer's powers of disposition.

If, however, a hirer allows a third party to become invested with rights over goods comprised in a hire-purchase agreement, the respective rights of the owner and the third party will depend on the special rules applicable to the disposition in question.

Following is an account of the more important dispositions, and of the special rules which govern them.

Sale

The general rule is that a buyer of goods let on hire-purchase will not acquire title as against the owner. The more important exceptional cases are as follows. First, sales in market overt are in the exceptional category. See, e.g., Bishopsgate Motor Finance Company Ltd. v. Transport Brakes Ltd. (1949) 1K.B.322. Secondly, certain sales by a dealer, of goods let to him on hire-purchase, are also exceptional. In question here are sales by a dealer, who holds goods under a stocking agreement with a finance company. Section 2(b), 1960 Act.

Thirdly, a person who buys goods, from a factor who holds the goods under a hire-purchase agreement, may be able to assert title as against the owner under Section 2, Factors Act, 1889.

It is also conceivable that an owner may be *estopped* from denying the title of a purchaser of goods let on hire-purchase.

Distress

A landlord may distrain goods, which are in the possession of a tenant under a hire-purchase agreement, in respect of arrears of rent. Section 4(1), Law of Distress Amendment Act, 1908. See, however, Section 17(2), 1946 Act. A clause in the hire-purchase agreement, which prohibits the tenant from suffering distraint, would not appear to bind a landlord who rightfully distrains.

Bankruptcy

In general terms, a hirer's bankruptcy has the effect of making goods held by the hirer on hire-purchase available for distribution among the hirer's creditors. See, e.g., sections 70 and 78 of the Bankruptcy Act, 1988. Although the matter has not been decided upon in the Irish courts, it seems that a clause which seeks to protect an owner from the effects of the above sections will be ineffective.

Liens

A repairer of goods let on hire-purchase may acquire a lien over them for any unpaid costs of the repairs. This lien will in general subsist against the owner of the goods, even where the hire-purchase agreement prohibits the creation of a lien, if the repairer was unaware of the prohibition.

Albermarle Supply Co. v. Hind (1928) 1 K.B. 307.
A taxicab operator acquired three taxicabs from the plaintiffs under hire-purchase agreements. He kept the cabs at the garage of the defendant, who maintained them in consideration of a rent. When the taxicab operator defaulted in the rent payments, the defendant claimed a lien over the

taxicabs. *Notwithstanding this claim, the defendant permitted the taxicab operator to remove the cabs on a daily basis on condition that the lien continue to subsist over them.*

The taxicab operator subsequently defaulted in his hire-purchase repayments to the plaintiffs, who brought an action against the garage owner, claiming the return of the cabs. It was held that the defendant was entitled to a possessory lien in respect of the vehicles, notwithstanding the agreement under which the taxicab operator had been permitted to use the cabs on a daily basis.

Assignment

A hirer may effectively assign his interest in a hire-purchase agreement to a third party, except where the agreement contains a clause prohibiting such assignment. See, e.g., *Belsize Motor Supply Co. v. Cox* (1914) 1 K.B. 244.

IMPLIED TERMS IN HIRE-PURCHASE AGREEMENTS

Certain terms are implied in every hire-purchase agreement by virtue of Part III of the Sale of Goods and Supply of Services Act, 1980, which repealed section 9, H.P.A., 1946. The relevant provisions, which are designed to correct the imbalance of bargaining power as between owners and hirers, seeks to place a hire-purchaser in much the same position as a buyer of goods as far as implied terms are concerned.

Account of the Terms

The implied terms will now be considered.

First, in general, there is an implied condition that the owner will have a right to sell the goods when the property in them is to pass, an implied warranty that the goods are free, and will remain free until the time when the property is to pass, from encumbrances, and also an implied warranty that the hire-purchaser will enjoy quiet possession of the goods. Section 26, S.G.S.S.A., 1980. See also, e.g., Karflex v Poole (1933)2 K.B. 251.

These terms are not however implied in a contract where it appears from the circumstances that the owner should transfer only such title as he may have. In the latter situation, however, there are implied warranties that the seller has disclosed any encumbrances known to him and, also, that neither he nor any third party who is privy with him will disturb the hire-purchaser's quiet possession to the extent to which title has been transfered.

Secondly, in a hire-purchase by description, there is an implied condition that the goods shall correspond with the description. If a hire-purchase by description should also be a hire-purchase by sample, it is not sufficient that the bulk of the goods corresponds with the sample if the goods do not also correspond with the description. Section 27, S.G.S.S.A., 1980.

Goods may be let by description notwithstanding that, being exposed for sale or hire, they are selected by the hirer.

Thirdly, where an owner lets goods under a hire-purchase agreement in the course of a business, there is an implied condition that the goods supplied are of merchantable quality, except that there is no such condition:—

"(a) As regards defects specifically drawn to the hirer's attention before the agreement is made, or (b) if the hirer examines the goods before the agreement is made, as regards defects which that examination ought to have revealed". Section 28(2), S.G.S.S.A., 1980.

An Bord Iascaigh Mhara v. Scallon, (1438-1970, H.Ct., Unrep., 8—5—1973)
The defendant had concluded a hire-purchase agreement with the plaintiffs for a fishing boat. The trawling equipment on board was not sufficiently powerful for normal trawling. There was a default in the payments and, when the plaintiff sued for arrears, the defendant counterclaimed for damages for breaches of the implied terms regarding merchantable quality and fitness for purpose. He failed on the first contention on the basis that the boat was fit for all purposes other than trawling. He succeeded, however, in his second contention. The court held that the plaintiffs were guilty of a breach of the statutory condition under Section 9(2), H.P.A., 1946.

Fourthly, a condition that goods let on hire-purchase are reasonably fit for a particular purpose is also implied under Section 28 (3), S.G.S.S.A., 1980, as follows:—

"Where the owner lets goods under a hire-purchase agreement in the course of a business and the hirer, expressly or by implication, makes known to the owner or the person by whom any antecedent negotiations (as defined in section 35) are conducted, any particular purpose for which the goods are being hired, there is an implied condition that the goods supplied under the agreement are reasonably fit for that purpose, whether or not that is a purpose for which such goods are commonly supplied, except where the circumstances show that the hirer does not rely, or that it is unreasonable for him to rely on the skill or judgment of the owner or that person".

A case decided under the previous version of this provision is Butterly v United Dominions Trust Ltd. (1963) I.R. 56.
See also, e.g., Yeoman Credit Ltd. v Apps (1961) 2 A.E.R. 281.

Fifthly, a number of conditions are implied in relation to hire-purchase by sample. The bulk must correspond with the sample in quality. Also, the hire-purchaser must be allowed a reasonable opportunity of comparing the bulk with the sample. In addition, a condition is implied whereby the bulk must be free from any defect that would make it unmerchantable, which defect would not be apparent on a reasonable examination of the sample. Section 29 S.G.S.S.A., 1980.

Sixthly, in a hire-purchase agreement, there are implied warranties that spare parts and an adequate aftersale service will be made available by the owner in such circumstances as are stated in any offer, description or advertisement by the owner on behalf of the manufacturer or on his own behalf. Section 33, S.G.S.S.A., 1980.

Seventhly, in every contract for the hire-purchase of a motor vehicle (except a contract in which the hire-purchaser is a person whose business it is to deal in motor vehicles), there is an implied condition that at the time of delivery of the vehicle under the contract it is free from any defect which would render it a danger to the public, including persons travelling in the vehicle. Section 34, S.G.S.S.A., 1980. This term can be excluded by an express agreement which is evidenced in writing and signed by the parties, provided that the agreement is fair and reasonable.

Exclusion of the Terms

The terms regarding title, freedom from encumbrances and quiet possession can in no instance be excluded.

The terms regarding correspondence with description, merchantable quality, fitness for purpose and correspondence with sample can not be excluded where the hire-purchaser *deals as consumer*. In other cases, these terms can be excluded by agreement, although such agreement will be unenforceable unless it is shown to be fair and reasonable. Section 31, S.G.S.S.A., 1980.

Liability arising from Antecedent Negotiations

Liability for the performance of a hire-purchase agreement (including liability for the implied terms) may not rest solely with the owner. The relevant provisions are Sections 32 and 35, S.G.S.S.A., 1980, and these also refer to the question of liability for misrepresentations made in the course of negotiations antecedent to the hire-purchase agreement. Section 32 is as follows:—

"Where goods are let under a hire-purchase agreement to a hirer dealing as consumer, the person, if any, by whom the antecedent negotiations (as defined in section 35) were conducted shall be deemed to be a party to the agreement and that person and the owner shall, jointly and severally, be answerable to the hirer for breach of the agreement and for any misrepresentations made by that person with respect to the goods in the course of the antecedent negotiations".

It bears emphasis that advantage can be taken of the above provision only where the hire-purchaser is *dealing as consumer.*

INEFFECTIVE TERMS IN HIRE-PURCHASE AGREEMENTS

The governing legislation protects hire-purchasers, not only by providing for certain implied terms in hire-purchase agreements, but also by providing that certain terms inserted by owners in such agreements shall be void. These *ineffective* terms will now be considered.

Entry on Premises

Any clause which gives an owner a right of entry on any premises for the purpose of taking possession of goods let on hire-purchase, or which relieves an owner from liability for such entry, is void. A qualified exception is made for hire-purchase agreements which relate to motor vehicles. Section 6 (a), H.P.A., 1946, as amended by section 16 (1), H.P.A.A. 1960.

Liability on Statutory Termination

Any clause which restricts a hire purchaser's statutory right to terminate an agreement, or which imposes on a hire-purchaser who so terminates a greater liability than that provided for in the Acts, is void. Section 6(b), H.P.A., 1946, and section 5, H.P.A., 1946 as amended by section 23, H.P.A.A., 1960.

Liability on Termination otherwise than under Statute

A hire-purchaser may terminate his agreement otherwise than by exercising the statutory right to do so. Such a termination could occur by virtue of a breach of the agreement, under the terms of the agreement or by operation of law. A clause may purport to regulate the liability for a hire-purchaser on a termination in any of these ways; such a clause is void if it seeks to impose a greater liability than that permitted on a statutory termination. Section 6(c), H.P.A., 1946.

Agents of the Hire Purchaser

Any clause whereby any person is to be deemed the agent of the hire-purchaser, when in fact such, person is acting on behalf of the owner in connection with the formation of the hire-purchase, agreement, is void. Section 6(d), H.P.A., 1946.

Agents of the Owner

Any clause whereby any person, who acts on behalf of the owner in connection with the formation of a hire-purchase agreement, is not to be deemed the agent of the owner, is void. Section 6(e), H.P.A., 1946.

OTHER TERMS IN HIRE-PURCHASE AGREEMENTS

Standardised hire-purchase agreements invariably contain express terms which are not regulated by the legislation. Such clauses relate, for example to maintenance prior to delivery to hirer, particulars as to delivery, maintenance by the hirer, and insurance by the hirer.

It is also worth noting that the exclusion of liability for breach of terms (whether express or implied) in hire-purchase agreements is subject to common law principles as well as to the statutory provisions on the matter. Thus, for instance, exclusion clauses are interpreted contra proferentem. See, for example, *Butterly v. United Dominions Trusts Ltd.* (1963) I.R. 57. Such clauses, moreover, may be ineffective to exclude liability for fundamental breaches of agreement. See, e.g., *Clayton Love Ltd. v. B. & I. Ltd.*, 104 I.L.T.R. 157, and *Photo-Productions Ltd. v Securicor Ltd.* (1980) 1 All E.R. 556.

LIABILITY FOR MISREPRESENTATIONS

A hirer may conclude a hire-purchase agreement in reliance on a misrepresentation not made a term of the agreement. Liability for such misrepresentation may be fixed either on its author or on some other person accountable for the statements of the author. The liability may be based either in contract or tort.

The triangular transaction provides an illustrative framework for considering the law on this topic. The problem arises in the context of the triangular transaction when a hirer concludes a hire-purchase agreement with a finance company in reliance on a misrepresentation made by a dealer.

Although there is now statutory regulation in this area — namely, Sections 32 and 35, S.G.S.S.A., 1980, which have already been discussed — the common law is still relevant, since the statutory provisions apply only where the hire-purchaser deals *as a consumer*.

Liability of the Dealer
The alternative bases for fixing liability on the dealer are threefold. First, he may be made liable for breach of a collateral contract.

Andrews v. Hopkinson (1957) 1 Q.B. 229. The defendant was a car dealer. He represented to the plaintiff that a particular car was in good condition, saying, — "It's a good little bus. I would stake my life on it. You will have no trouble with it". Subsequently, a hire-purchase agreement was arranged with a finance company and the plaintiff paid a deposit to the company. One week later, the plaintiff was injured in an accident which was attributed to a defect in the car's steering. The plaintiff recovered damages from the dealer, both for the diminution in value of the car, and for personal injury.

Secondly, the dealer may be liable in tort under the doctrine of *Hedley Byrne & Co. Ltd. v. Heller & Partners Ltd.*, 1964 A.C. 465. The doctrine in that case, which governs liability for innocent misrepresenations, was approved in *Securities Trust Ltd. v. Moore & Alexander Ltd.* (1964) I.R. 417. Thirdly, the dealer may be liable for the tort of deceit if the misrepresentation was fraudulent. See, e.g., *Derry v. Peek* (1889) 14 App. Cas. 337, and *Lombank Ltd. v. MacElligott & Sons Ltd.* 99 I.L.T.R. 9.

Liability of the Finance Company

A finance company can generally not be held vicariously liable for a dealer's misrepresentations, since a dealer has independent contractor status.

Any accountability of a finance company must rest on agency principles. The liability of a principal for the misrepresentations (innocent or fraudulent) of an agent is established. *Bank of Ireland v. Smith* (1966) I.R. 646.

The problem lies in proving the relationship of the principal and agent between the finance company and the dealer. The case-law provides that, while there is no presumption of agency, the facts in a particular case may warrant a finding of agency. See, e.g., *Mercantile Credit Co. Ltd. v. Hamblin* (1964) 3 All E.R. 492, and *Financings Ltd. v. Stinson* (1963) 3 All E.R. 386.

HIRE-PURCHASE FINANCING

The instalment payment system in hire-purchase poses difficulties of maintaining liquidity for many dealers. These difficulties can often be overcome only with the assistance of finance companies, which can supply the credit element in the transaction.

Such companies finance practically all hire-purchase and credit sale transactions in motor vehicles, and in agricultural and industrial machinery. They also finance the bulk of the credit transactions involving radios and television sets. On the other hand, the majority of credit transactions involving other items of domestic equipment - such as cookers, stoves and fridges - are conducted through the trading concerns dealing in these goods.

Following are the principal arrangements where by dealers and finance companies combine to provide goods on hire-purchase:—

Hire-Purchase Agreement with Permissory Note
A hirer may be required to sign a promissory note for the hire-purchase price as well as the hire-purchase agreement. The dealer can immediately negotiate the note to the finance company for cash. See, e.g., *Modern Light Cars Ltd. v. Seals,* (1934) 1 K.B. 32.

Block Discounting
A dealer, by arrangement, may regularly assign the benefits of a block of hire-purchase agreements to a finance company at a discount. See, e.g., *Olds Discount Co. Ltd. v. John Playfair, Ltd.* (1938) 3 All E.R. 375.

Stocking Agreements
A finance company may assist a dealer in stocking. For example, the finance company may purchase the stock, let them to the dealer on hire-purchase and the dealer in turn can let them on hire-purchase.

Triangular Transaction
The dealer, under this type of agreement, sells goods which are to be let to a finance company. It is the finance company which concludes the hire-purchase agreement with the hirer.

Recent Developments
The triangular transaction, which is the most common method by which finance companies

participate in hire-purchase, has begun to prove unpopular with the finance companies. This method carries the disadvantage for the finance companies of bringing them into privity of hire-purchase contract with the hirer, and so of rendering them liable on the terms implied by statute — in particular, the terms implied by Sections 26—35, S.G.S.S.A., 1980, (formerly Section 9, 1946 Act).

The finance companies have therefore devised new methods of participating with dealers in providing goods on credit to consumers. The principal method is for the finance company to advance a loan to the consumer, which loan is secured by a promissory note providing for repayment by instalments. The advance is used to conclude an outright sale with the dealer. This more recent type of transaction involves, as can be seen, no element of hire-purchase.

TERMINATION OF HIRE-PURCHASE AGREEMENTS AND MINIMUM PAYMENT CLAUSES

It has long been the practice for owners of goods let on hire-purchase to insert minimum payment clauses in their agreements with hirers. These clauses provide that, on the termination of hire-purchase agreements, a sum additional to the arrears of instalments shall be payable by the hirer. This additional sum may be justified (and described) either as compensation for depreciation, as liquidated damages or as a recompense for loss of profits.

Abuse of the minimum payment clause device is presently regulated by a number of principles, both statutory and common law. The relevant principle in any given case will depend on the manner in which a hire-purchase agreement has been determined.

Termination under Hirer's Statutory Right

Any hire-purchase agreement, other than one in respect of industrial plant and machinery where the cash price exceeds £200, may be determined by the hirer under statute. Section 5, 1946 Act, as amended by Section 23, 1960 Act.

The amount payable by the hirer on a statutory determination, apart from any sum that may have become owing prior to the determination on foot of a breach of agreement, is determined by reference to what can, in general terms, be described as a *50 per cent formula.* Under this formula, the hirer can be required to pay any arrears and such further sum, if any, as will bring his payments up to one half of the hire-purchase price. Section 5, 1946 Act. Where an installation by the owner is provided for under a hire-purchase agreement, the 50 per cent formula will be modified to take account of installation charges in accordance with Section 19, 1946 Act. Moreover, if the agreement provides for a sum less than that payable under 50 per cent formula to be payable on a statutory termination, the lesser sum shall be payable.

The statutory minimum payment clause, based on the 50 per cent formula, applies *directly* only to a termination of a hire-purchase agreement under the hirer's statutory right. The statutory formula is, however, also posited as a *maximum* ceiling for any minimum payment clause contained in a hire-purchase agreement which terminates otherwise than by the exercise of the hirer's statutory right:—

"Any provision in any agreement whereby a hirer, after the determination of the hire-purchase agreement or the bailment in any manner whatsoever, is subject to a liability which exceeds the liability to which he would have been subject if the agreement had been determined by him under this Act ... shall be void." Section 6(c), 1946 Act".

Termination by Hirer's Breach of Agreement

The owner may determine a hire-purchase agreement on foot of a breach by the hirer of a condition contained in the agreement. A contractual minimum payment clause, designed to be operative in such event, may be enforced if the amount payable under it represents a genuine pre-estimate of the owner's loss (i.e., liquidated damages). Such a clause will not, however, be enforceable if it is punitive rather than compensatory in nature. See, e.g., *Dunlop Pneumatic Tyre Co. Ltd. v. New Garage and Motor Co. Ltd.* (1915) A.C. 79; 83 L.J.K.B. 1574, H.L.

Termination under Terms of Agreement

It is common for hire-purchase agreements to confer a right of termination on the hirer. The hirer can exercise the right by returning the goods and by paying the amount prescribed in the minimum payment clause where one exists. Although the question does not appear to have been considered by the Irish courts, or to have been decided by the House of Lords, it would seem that the minimum payment clause may be enforceable in such cirsumstances, even where it does not represent a genuine pre-estimate of the owner's loss. See, e.g., *Campbell Discount Co. Ltd. v. Bridge* (1961) 2 All E.R. 97, C.A.

Termination by Operation of Law

A hire-purchase agreement may terminate by operation of law, e.g., on the death or bankruptcy (liquidation in the case of a company) of the hirer. On existing authority, a minimum payment clause could be enforced on a termination in such circumstances, notwithstanding that the clause embodies a penalty element. *Re Apex Supply Co. Ltd.* (1942) Ch. 108. See, however, *Bridge v Campbell Discount Co. Ltd.* (1962) A.C. 600.

Guarantees

Security means freedom from worry.

Banker's Adage.

CHAPTER III : GUARANTEES

A guarantee is an undertaking to be collaterally responsible for the debt, default, or miscarriage of another. The transaction is highly adaptable, and a guarantee may be ancillary to contracts of, for example, employment, loan or sale of goods.

Guarantee law is primarily judge-made. The common law rules developed to govern the relations between the parties to a guarantee reflect a judicial leaning in favour of the guarantor as against the creditor. The rights of a guarantor at common law may however be expressly excluded, and such exclusion is common in the standard guarantees used by professional lenders.

Although the term *guarantee* in its traditional sense denotes a secondary and contingent liability, a second usage of the term has emerged in recent years to denote an *additional* liability. Thus, in certain retail trades - such as in the sale of motor vehicles and consumer electrical products - manufacturers and suppliers undertake liabilities additional to those of the seller. Guarantees thus given by manufacurers and suppliers are now governed by the Sale of Goods and Supply of Services Act, 1980.

Finally, mention can be made of a proposed E.E.C. directive on guarantee and indemnity. This directive deals with such matters as capacity to guarantee, the role of writing and the proper law of guarantees which involve a transnational element.

GUARANTEES AT COMMON LAW

GUARANTEE DISTINGUISHED FROM INDEMNITY

The characteristics of a guarantee are threefold. First, there are three parties concerned and two contracts. Secondly, a guarantor's liability, since it arises only on the default of the party responsible on the primary contract, is secondary. Thirdly, a guarantor will have no direct financial interest in the primary contract. See, e.g., *Sutton & Co. v. Grey* (1894) 1 Q.B. 285.

A guarantee should be distinguished from an indemnity, since only the former need be in writing. Both transactions will be ancillary to a primary contract. An indemnifier however, unlike a guarantor, accepts primary responsibility on the primary contract. The distinction between a guarantee and an indemnity was explained as follows in the early but well-known case of *Birkmyr v Darnell* (1704) 1 Salk 27:– If A says to C, *"Let B have the goods, and if he does not pay you, I will"*, the subsequent contract will be a guarantee. Conversely, if A says, *"Give B the goods, I will be your paymaster"*, the subsequent contract is an indemnity.

LEGAL REQUIREMENTS OF A GUARANTEE

A guarantee, like any other contract, is made when there is an offer by one party which is accepted by another party.

The ensueing agreement must be supported by consideration or, alternatively, be under seal. An undertaking to grant further advance will be adequate consideration for a guarantee in respect, not only of the further advances, but also of advances previously made. *Provincial Bank of Ireland Ltd. v. O'Donnell,* C.A. (1934) N.I.

An intention to create legal relations must also subsist between the parties to a guarantee.

Finally, a guarantee must be evidenced in writing and signed by the guarantor or his authorised agent. Sections 2 and 3 of the Statute of Frauds (Ire.) Act, 1695. The relevant provision of Section 2 is as follows:—

"No action shall be brought ... whereby to charge the defendant upon any special promise to answer for the debt, default or miscarriage of another person ... unless the agreement upon which such action shall be brought, or some memorandum or note thereof, shall be in writing and signed by the party to be charged therewith or some other person thereunto by him lawfully authorized."

The writing need not set out the consideration. Section 3, Mercantile Law Amendment Act, 1856. A verbal guarantee, although valid, is unenforceable.

CAPACITY TO GUARANTEE

Capacity to guarantee is co-extensive with capacity to contract generally. A company, for example, can give an enforceable guarantee only if empowered to do so in its memorandum. An infant, in general, lacks capacity to guarantee. Moreover, a guarantee ancillary to a primary contract to which an infant is a party, where the primary contract is void owing to the infant's capacity, is void. See, e.g., *Coutts & Co. v. Browne Lecky* (1947) K.B. 104.

Only in one case is a female guarantor in a different position from that of a male guarantor, namely, when she guarantees the account of her husband or of some company in which he is interested. The relationship of husband and wife does not in itself raise the *presumption* of undue influence. Nevertheless, it may be proved in a particular case that a husband did stand in a relation of dominion in obtaining a guarantee from his wife. In such event, the party seeking to sustain the transaction must rebut any presumption, arising from the facts, of undue influence.

PROCEDURAL ASPECTS OF GUARANTEES

The value of a guarantee depends on the ability of the guarantor to honour the liability. Professional creditors, therefore, seek to ascertain the financial position of a proposed guarantor.

In obtaining a guarantee, professional creditors seek also to ensure that the guarantor will not be capable of avoiding liability by means of either the defence of non est factum or of undue influence.

The above matters will now be considered.

Status Report
A guarantee by a person who lacks the funds to honour it is illusory. To ensure the value of a proferred guarantee, banks commonly seek a status report on the prospective guarantor from the latter's bank. Similar reports may be requested at regular intervals during the continuance of a guarantee in order that a realistic appraisal of its value be maintained.

If the creditor is a bank, and the proposed guarantor is one of its customers, no difficulty arises in obtaining a status report. In other circumstances, however, it is customary to inform the proposed guarantor that it is proposed to write to his bankers for their opinion as to his suitability to act as guarantor.

Undue Influence
A guarantor may avoid liability under a guarantee by pleading that it was given under undue influence. This plea will succeed if the undue influence was exerted by the principal debtor (who would not be a party to the guarantee). See, e.g., *Lancashire Loans Ltd. v. Black* (1934) 1 K.B. 380.

Certain relationships - such as, solicitor and client, trustee and beneficiary - raise a presumption of undue influence. The relationship of husband and wife does not, although little evidence is required to establish it.

There are two main ways in which a creditor may seek to offset the possibility of the defence of undue influence where the principal debtor and the prospective guarantor are in a suspect relationship. First, it can require that the proposed guarantor take independant legal advice. Secondly, it can require the proposed guarantor to sign - in addition to the guarantee itself - a statement to the effect that he has read the guarantee, that he understands it, and that he signs it voluntarily.

Non est factum

This plea is available to one who becomes party to a document under a mistaken belief as to its character or contents, where that belief has been induced by another's misrepresentation. Thus, if a principal debtor procures a guarantee by misrepresenting the character or contents of the document which is signed, the guarantor can avoid liability unless he has been careless in signing. See, e.g., *Carlisle and Cumberland Banking Co. v. Bragg* (1911) 1 K.B. 489; and *Gallie v. Lee* (1971) A.C. 1004.

A creditor can safeguard against the plea of *non est factum* by requiring that the guarantee be signed in the presence of, for example, a bank official or of some other responsible person, such as a solicitor.

UBERRIMAE FIDEI IS NOT REQUIRED

A creditor has no duty of disclosure when securing a guarantor, except when the guarantee is one of fidelity. If a fidelity guarantee is to be enforceable, all material facts must be disclosed prior to its conclusion. See, e.g., *London General Omnibus Co. v. Holloway* (1912) 2 K.B. 72.

Although generally not *uberrimae fidei*, contracts of guarantee will be unenforceable if procured by misrepresentation, whether innocent or fraudulent. See, e.g., *Northern Banking Co. v. Mordaunt* 60 I.L.T.R. 129; and *Northern Bank Finance Corporation Ltd. v. Charlton, Charlton and Sheehy.* (1979) I.R. 149.

Macken v. Munster & Leinster Bank Ltd. & O'Grady (1961) I.L.T.R. 19
In this case, the principal debtor, when applying for a loan from the defendant, represented that he had sufficient security in Holland to meet his commitments. This representation was never verified by the bank. The plaintiff agreed to go guarantor on the loan, relying on the assurance by an official of the defendant bank that the principal debtor's foreign assets made him creditworthy. Subsequently, the principal debtor defaulted, and it was discovered that he had no property abroad. The court granted the declaration sought by the plaintiff that he was not liable as guarantor, on the basis that the guarantee had been induced by a negligent misrepresentation.

TERMS OF A GUARANTEE

A guarantee may consist simply of an undertaking to accept secondary liability on a transaction. However, the standard guarantee of professional lenders are lengthy documents which regulate many facets of the relationships between the creditor, the principal debtor and the guarantor.

Following is an outline of the main terms commonly found in standard guarantees.

Operative Clause

The following typifies the operative clause in a guarantee where the primary obligation is secured by one person only:— *"I, the undersigned, A, hereby guarantee payment to you on demand of the monies advanced by you to D".*

More than one person may guarantee the same primary obligation. One example is where a club borrows to further its objectives - the borrowing may be guaranteed by a number of club members. Another common example is where partners guarantee an obligation undertaken by their firm.

A guarantee which involves two or more co-guarantors can take any one of three forms, and the operative clause will vary depending on the form adopted. First, each co-guarantor may give a separate guarantee. Secondly, all the co-guarantors may give one joint guarantee. The operative clause in such event would read as follows:— *"We, the undersigned, A, B and C, hereby jointly guarantee payment, etc.".*

76

Thirdly, all the co-guarantors may give one joint and several guarantee. The operative clause here would read as follows:— *"We, the undersigned, A, B and C, hereby jointly and severally guarantee payment, etc".* Professional lenders - such as banks - almost invariably use this third form of guarantee. Since the co-guarantors adopt joint and several liability, an unsatisfied judgment obtained against one will not preclude an action against the other(s).

Duration of Guarantee: Specific or Continuing

It is usual to specify the duration of a guarantee. In this context, a broad distinction can be drawn between specific and continuing guarantees.

A specific guarantee covers only a specified transaction, and it is determined by reference to that transaction. A continuing guarantee, in contrast, is one which extends to a series of transactions, and which is not exhausted by, or confined to, a single credit or transaction. Whether a guarantee is specific or continuing depends on the intention of the parties as found in the language of the contract, and in the surrounding circumstances. See, e.g.; *Hargreave v. Smee* (1829) 6 Bing. 244; *Kay v. Groves* (1829) 6 Bing. 276; and *Northern Banking Co. v. Mordaunt,* 60 I.L.T.R. 129.

The standard guarantees of professional lenders - such as banks - are almost invariably continuing. This is normally expressed in such phrase as the following:— *"And I hereby declare that this guarantee is to be a continuing guarantee until the expiration of three calendar months after the receipt by you from me of notice in writing to discontinue it".*

Enforcement of the Guarantee

A standard guarantee will normally contain provisions relating to its enforcement. These may simply be declaratory of the common law; an example would be a provision that the creditor may seek payment from the guarantor, without first seeking by litigation to enforce payment from the principal debtor.

Provisions on enforcement, moreover, commonly remove certain defences available to a guarantor at common law. For example, the creditor may reserve the right to enforce the guarantee notwithstanding that the terms of the primary obligation have been altered, that the composition of the parties has altered or that securities taken from the principal debtor have been released.

RIGHTS OF THE GUARANTOR

A guarantee invests the guarantor with secondary liability for the obligation of the principal debtor. This secondary liability is contingent on the default of the principal debtor, and also on the creditor's compliance with any preconditions to the guarantee.

Mahon v. Irish National Insurance Co. (1958) Ir. Jur. 41.
The defendant, an insurance company, issued a

guarantee bond pursuant to Section 14 of the Auctioneers and Estate Agents Act, 1947, guaranteeing the performance of the obligations incurred by an auctioneer. The plaintiff, when the auctioneer had defaulted in his obligations, recovered judgment against him. When this judgement was not satisfied, he proceeded against the insurance company as guarantor. The action failed. Under the 1947 Act, a precondition to liability is the giving of notice to the insurer of the institution of any proceedings against the auctioneer. The plaintiff had neglected to fulfill this requirement.

A guarantee imposes a contingent liability on the guarantor, but it also invests him with rights against the creditor, the principal debtor and co-guarantors. These rights will now be considered.

Rights against the Creditor

First, the guarantor has the right to be informed of the extent of his liability at any particular time. Secondly, he has the right to demand that the creditor seek payment from the principal debtor after the debt has become due. He cannot however compel the creditor to sue for payment, unless the guarantee provides otherwise. *Wright v. Simpson* (1802) 6 Ves. 714.

Thirdly, the guarantor, if sued by the creditor, can avail of any defences or set-off which would have been available to the principal debtor. Thus, for example, the guarantor may plead that the primary obligation has been statute-barred. Fourthly, the guarantor, after he has satisifed his undertaking, can compel the creditor either:– (a). to allow his name to be used as plaintiff in an action brought by the guarantor against the principal debtor, or (b). to assign the benefit of the primary obligation to him (the guarantor) for the purpose of bringing such action.

Fifthly, after he has paid the creditor, the guarantor becomes subrogated to all the rights of the creditor in respect of the debt. Section 3, Mercantile Law Amendment Act, 1856. He can, for example, sue the principal debtor.

He is also entitled to the benefit of any securities given by the principal debtor to the creditor.

Royal Bank of Ireland v. Smith and Smith 61 I.L.T.R. 61.
The defendants agreed verbally to guarantee the principal debtor to the extent of £4,000. It was a precondition to this agreement that the principal debtor would deposit title deeds as security. The bank never obtain this security. The defendants later signed a letter of guarantee on being assured that it was "as arranged". The letter of guarantee contained no reference to the security. An action by the bank to enforce the written agreement failed. The court held that the letter of guarantee should be rectified, and that the value of the securities should be credited to the guarantors.

The guarantor's right to securities extends even to any of which he was unaware when giving the guarantee. The right also exists in respect of securities received by the creditor after the date of the guarantee. See, e.g., *Forbes v. Jackson* (1882) 19 Ch. D. 615; and *Northern Banking Co. v. Newman and Calton* (1927) I.R. 520.

Where a guarantor has guaranteed only part of a debt, his rights to the securities are partial only.

Sixthly, a guarantor in the case of a fidelity guarantee has a special right. If he knows that an employee whose conduct is guaranteed has misconducted himself so as to make him liable for dismissal, he can compel the employer either to dismiss the employee or to forfeit the benefit of the guarantee. See, e.g., *Philips v. Foxall* (1872) L.R., 7 Q.B. 666.

Rights against the Principal Debtor

First, the guarantor can require the principal debtor to pay the creditor as soon as the debt becomes due; he can, moreover, obtain an order compelling the debtor to pay. See, e.g., *Tate v. Crewdson* (1938) Ch. 869. Secondly, after he has paid the creditor the guarantor is entitled to be indemnified by the principal debtor. This right to indemnity may be implied or express. It is implied where the guarantee has been undertaken at the principal debtor's request.

Thirdly, the guarantor, if sued by the creditor, can issue a third party notice to the principal debtor. This notice - which is a procedural device for consolidating two or more causes of action - makes the debtor a party to the proceedings.

Rights against Co-Guarantors

First, a guarantor who has paid more than his share of a common liability is entitled to contribution from his co-guarantors. The right to contribution is equitable as distinct from contractual. It applies whether the co-guarantors are bound by the same or by different instructions, and it applies whether or not the guarantor seeking contribution knew of the existence of the co-guarantors when he became liable.

The right to contribution does not arise however in the following circumstances:—

a.　where the co-guarantors have guaranteed equal portions of the same debt;

b.　against a co-guarantor who undertook liability at the request of the guarantor seeking contribution; or

c.　where it is clear from surrounding circumstances that no right to contribution was intended.

Secondly, in order to obtain contribution, a guarantor who has paid more than his share of the common liability must bring into account all securities received by him in respect of his payment. See, e.g., *Re Acredeckne* (1883) Ch. D. 709.

RIGHTS OF THE CREDITOR

The basic right of the creditor is to obtain the performance of the principal debtor on the primary contract.

If the debtor defaults, the creditor may realise any securities held by him. He can - in addition or in the alternative - proceed against the guarantor.

RIGHTS OF THE PRINCIPAL DEBTOR

The principal debtor, after he has performed the primary contract, can recover any securities held by the creditor.

DISCHARGE OF THE GUARANTOR

A guarantor will be discharged in the circumstances set out below.

Payment
In the case of a specific guarantee, discharge of the guarantor normally occurs on the repayment of the loan by the principal debtor. A guarantor can also be discharged by payment in satisfaction of his undertaking.

Effluxion of Time
A guarantee for a fixed period is discharged at the end of the set period. A continuing guarantee is discharged on the expiry of notice given under it. Standard bank guarantees usually provide for

a notice period of three months.

Variation of the Parties

In the absence of a provision to the contrary, a variation of the parties will discharge the guarantor. For example, if the principal debtor is a partnership, a variation in the composition of the firm will discharge the guarantor.

Discharge in this way will also occur if any co-guarantor is released from liability by the creditor without the consent of the other co-guarantors. The mere withdrawal of an action against one co-guarantor will not however discharge the others.

Watkins, Jameson and Pim Ltd. v. Stacey and Harding Ltd. (1961) 95 I.L.T.R. 122.
The plaintiff took proceedings for damages for the breach by the first-named defendants of a repairing covenant. The second and third-named defendants had co-guaranteed the performance of the lease agreement. While the action was being heard, the plaintiffs withdrew their action against one guarantor, whereupon one of the other co-guarantors sought to be discharged. He was unsuccessful. His rights had not been prejudiced in any way, as the withdrawal of the action did not diminish the liability of the guarantor in respect of whom the action had been discontinued.

Release or Variation of the Primary Obligation

A guarantor will be discharged if the creditor releases the principal debtor under the primary obligation.

Similarly, a discharge will result if there is any variation in the terms of the primary obligation without the consent of the guarantor, provided that the variation is to the detriment of the latter. An example, would be where the creditor, under a legal agreement, allows additional time for payment of the principal debtor. See, e.g., *Provincial Bank of Ireland v. Fisher* (1919) 2 I.R. 249; and *Midland Motor Showroom v. Newman* (1929) 2 K.B. 256.

Release or Loss of the Securities

If the creditor releases securities held from the principal debtor, this operates to discharge the guarantor to the extent of the securities released. See, e.g., *Northern Banking Co. v. Newman and Calton* (1927) I.R. 520.

Similarly, a failure by the creditor to protect securities held from the principal debtor will discharge the guarantor to the extent to which his rights are affected. See, e.g., *Wulff and Billing v. Jay* (1877) L.R. 7 Q.B. 756.

Gross Negligence of the Creditor

The guarantor may be discharged if the failure to perform on the primary obligation is attributable in part to the gross negligence of the creditor. Discharge could occur in this way, for example, if the wrongdoing of an employee, whose conduct has been guaranteed, has been facilitated by the employer's failure to exercise proper supervision. See, e.g., *Fraher v. County Council of Waterford* (1926) I.R. 505.

Death, Incapacity or Bankruptcy

The death, incapacity or bankruptcy of either the principal debtor or the guarantor can operate to discharge the guarantee. The operative date is when the creditor obtains notice of any such event.

MANUFACTURERS AND SUPPLIERS GUARANTEES

EXPLANATION

The undertaking given under a manufacturer's or a supplier's guarantee is normally additional - as distinct from secondary - to that given by the seller.

Such guarantees are, in essence, viewed by the guarantors as marketing devices. A number of sharp practices had formerly attended their use. The scope of the guarantee, for example, was frequently not defined. Also, in return for the guarantee, the purchaser might be required to sign a form which would effectively surrender his common law and statutory rights under the sale transaction. In addition, the mode of redress under the guarantee was often not specified.

REGULATION

Manufacturers' and suppliers' guarantees are now subject to regulation under the Sale of Goods and Supply of Services Act, 1980. This defines the type of guarantee with which it is concerned as:—

"Any document, notice or other statement, however described, supplied by a manufacturer

or other supplier, other than a retailer, in connection with the supply of any goods and indicating that the manufacutrer or other supplier will service, repair or otherwise deal with the goods following purchase". Section 15.

Such guarantees must be clearly legible and must refer only to specific goods or to one category of goods. They must contain certain minimum information, including the following:—

a.   The name and address of the person supplying the guarantee.

b.   The duration of the guarantee.

c.   The claims procedure.

d.   A clear statement of what the manufacturer or other supplier undertakes to do in relation to the goods and, also, of any charges that may be imposed on the buyer.

The omission of the above information from a regulated guarantee is an offence. Section 16.

The following additional regulation of suppliers' and manufacturers' guarantees is also contained in the Act. First, a seller of goods who delivers a guarantee to the buyer shall be liable to the buyer for the observance of its terms as if he were the guarantor. There are two exceptional cases. The first is where the seller expressly indicates to the buyer, at the time of delivery of the guarantee, that he will not be liable for its observance. The second exceptional case is where the seller, being a retailer, gives the buyer his own written undertaking that he will service, repair or otherwise deal with the goods following purchase; it will be presumed in this situation, unless the contrary is proved, that the seller has not made himself liable to the buyer under the guarantee. Section 17.

Secondly, rights under a guarantee shall not exclude or limit the buyer's statutory or common law rights. Neither shall they impose on the buyer obligations additional to those in his contract. Section 18(1). Thirdly, any provision in a guarantee which gives the seller or his agent sole power to decide whether or not goods are defective, or to decide whether the buyer is otherwise entitled to present a claim, shall be void. Section 18(2).

Finally, various facets of the right of action under a guarantee are regulated. Section 19. Thus, breach of any term in a guarantee can be treated as a breach of warranty. Moreover, all persons who acquire title to the goods during the guaranteed period — and not only the original buyer — may sue on the guarantee.

Consumer Information Act, 1978

I only ask for information.

David Copperfield

CHAPTER IV: CONSUMER INFORMATION ACT, 1978

The Consumer Information Act, 1978, is relevant to all sections of the business community and, in consequence, to all consumers. Its effect, in broad terms, is to increase the level of accuracy required for information given in relation to the supply of goods or the provision of services.

The Act amends the Merchandise Marks Acts, 1887-1972. That legislation, although frequently revised since the Principal Act of 1887, was seen to require considerable updating in order to meet modern trading conditions. The earlier Acts contained, for example, a narrow notion of trade description - statements about only the more obvious characteristics, such as weight and measurements, were comprehended. The revised notice of trade description includes virtually all kinds of statements about goods which might influence a purchaser. The new Act, moreover, prohibits misleading, as well as false, statements. Finally, whereas the 1887 Act dealt only with trade descriptions that were on, with or near the goods, the new Act provides that information given verbally, or in an advertisement, or indeed in any other way, may be a trade description, and so subject to the required degree of truth and accuracy.

The present Act follows closely, in many respects, the British Trade Description Act, 1968.

One significant departure lies in the provision whereby a court, after imposing a fine for one of the specified offences, may order that the whole or part of the fine be paid in compensation to a consumer injured by the offence.

The unusually wide definition of *goods* in the legislation deserves mention; that term includes ships, vehicles and aircraft, land, things attached to land, and growing crops. Section 1.

THE OFFENCES

The primary offences created by the Act aim only at information provided in the course of trade or business. They cannot, therefore, be committed by an individual who is selling goods or supplying a service on a once-off basis.

The offences can be considered under six headings:—

False Trade Descriptions

It is an offence, in the course of any trade, business or profession, to apply a false description to any goods, or to supply or offer to supply any goods to which a false description is applied. Section 2, 3 and 5 of the Merchandise Marks, Act 1887, as amended by Section 2, 3 and 4 of the Consumer Information Act, 1978. These offences may be committed inadvertently, although it will be seen later that certain defences are available.

Beckett v. Kingston Brothers (Butchers) Ltd. (1970) 1 All E.R. 715.
The defendant company, having received a consignment of turkeys in bags labelled "Norfolk King Turkeys", dispatched them to its various outlets. When the turkeys were later discovered to be of Danish origin, notification to re-label them was sent to the company's shop managers. One manager disregarded the notification, and the company was prosecuted after a turkey had been sold under the incorrect label. The defence raised, namely, that the offence was caused by "an act or default of another person" proved successful.

The wide definition of trade description applicable to these offences covers, it would seem, almost every conveivable descriptive reference to goods. References to size, weight, origin and mode of manufacture are some examples. Section 2(1). A trade description is *false* in this context if it is false or misleading to a material degree. Section 2(2)(a).

False Statements as to Services, Accommodation or Facilities

The inclusion within the Act of provisions on false statements regarding services, accommodation and facilities probably represents the most novel advance on the earlier legislation. It is now an offence to make, in the course or for the purposes of a trade, business or profession, a false statement relating to services, accommodation or facilities. Section 6. The term *false* means false to a material degree.

The offence is committed only where the author of a statement knows of, or is reckless as to, it's falsity.

The British experience illustrates the potential catchment of this offence. Prosecutions have been brought against, for example, travel agents in respect of their holiday brochures, a motor trader in respect of his company's use of the word *guaranteed*, and against a builder in respect of his promise to build to specifications within a specified time. One surprising possibility to have emerged is that of multiple prosecutions arising from the one false statement. See, e.g., *R. v. Thomson Holidays Ltd.* (1974) 1 All E.R. 823.

False or Misleading Indications of Prices or Charges
A range of offences centres around prices and charges. Section 7. It is now an offence to give a false or misleading indication of prices or charges in the promotion of goods, services or accommodation.

The Act contains specific provisions on marked-down prices. Indications as to the former price are to connote, unless the contrary is expressed, that the goods, services or accommodation involved were offered openly at that price at the same place within the proceeding three months for not less than twenty eight successive days.

House of Holland v. London Borough of Brent (1971) 2 All E.R. 296.
The defendant had offered sun chair beds at the

*price of £2.5.0 in an advertisement indicating that "all prices further reduced". This indication was proved false, but only by reference to the prices offered within a period of two months preceding the advertisement. * An acquital resulted.*

The Act also focuses on recommended prices. A recommended price is to be treated as an indication of a price recommended by the producer, or other supplier for retail supply of the goods involved in the area where they are offered. This again, as in relation ot the statutory signification of marked-down prices, is in the absence of an expression to the contrary.

Misleading Advertisements

It is an offence to publish or cause to be published a misleading advertisement in relation to the promotion of goods, services or facilities. Section 8. Only advertisements inserted in the course of a trade, business or profession are covered.

An advertisement is misleading in this context if it is likely to mislead and thereby cause loss, damage or injury to members of the public to a material degree.

Contravention of Ministerial Orders

Contravention of marking orders or of advertising orders made by the Minister for Industry, Commerce and Tourism constitutes another class of offences under the Act. Section 10 and 11. Both of these types of order may be made if and when the Minister considers it necessary or expedient in the interest of consumers. A marking order can require that goods be marked with or accompanied by specified information or instructions. The information required could refer, for example, to the care, maintenance, storage or installation of the goods. '

The inclusion of similar relevant information in advertisements may be required by advertising orders. Such orders may be made in respect, not only of goods, but also of services, accommodation or facilities. '

The Minister also has power to make definition orders. Section 12. These can be used to assign definite meanings to words or expressions used in relation to the promotion of goods, services, accommodation or facilities. It is envisaged that definition orders might be used to assign meanings to words such as *pure, guaranteed* and *genuine.* The misuse in a business context of a word or phrase governed by a definition order would not, in its own right, constitute an offence; it could however be an element in one of the offences set out in the Act, such as the supply of goods to which a false description has been applied.

Miscellaneous Offences

A number of miscellaneous offences created by the Act remain for consideration. One such offence bears on retailers who sell food by weight. These are required to provide a weighing facility in a prominent position in a part of their premises to which the public have access. Any person who is buying food by weight must be permitted to observe the weighing of his purchase. Section 14.

A further offence safeguards the right to make price comparisons. Section 15. A person may not without reasonable cause be prevented from entering a place, where goods are offered for sale in the course of any trade or business, for the purpose of reading the prices of the goods. The phrase *"without reasonable cause"* would presumably justify a trader in refusing admission or the right of inspecting prices to, for example, a person who is merely loitering in or about the premises.

Finally, the obstruction or impeding of investigations conducted under the Act completes the litany of offences created by the legislation. Section 13(3) and Section 16(4).

PROSECUTIONS

Prosecutions for offences under the Act may be brought by the Minister for Industry, Commerce and Tourism, the Director of Consumer Affairs or by the local authority of the county or other borough in which an offence is alleged to have been committed. Section 9(6)(H) and Section 18(1).

The powers of prosecution granted represent for the Minister and for many local authorities simply an extension of powers held by them under previous Merchandise Marks legislation.

DEFENCES

The important topic of defences falls next for mention. 'An umbrella defence, available to a person charged with *any* of the offences referred to in the Act, is to prove:— (a). that the offence was due to a mistake, or to a reliance on information supplied to him, or to the act or default of another person, an accident or some other cause beyond his control; and (b) that he took all reasonable precautions and exercised all due diligence to avoid the commission of the offence by himself or any person under his control. Section 22(1).

> *Tesco Supermarkets v. Nattrass (1972) A.C. 153, H.L.*
> *The appellant, a public company which owned several hundred supermarkets, was charged with giving a false indication of a price at one of its branches. The offending window advertisement had stated that a particular washing powder was being sold at 2s. 11d. instead of the normal price of 3s. 11d. This advertisement remained on display when, after all the specially priced packets had been sold, an assistant had re-stocked the shelves with packets marked at the normal price. The branch manager concerned had, moreover, without seeking verification, noted in his check list that "All special offers O.K."*
>
> *The House of Lords acquitted the appellant company. The offence had been committed*

by "another person", since, owing to the size of its enterprise, the company was not to be identified with the branch manager directly responsible; and the system for avoiding offences which existed satisfied the requirments that due care and diligence be exercised.

The Act provides defences in respect of the offences which turn on the application of a false description to goods, and on the supply of such goods. Thus, the person charged can show that he had neither actual nor constructive knowledge of either the fact that the goods did not conform to the description or the fact that the description had been applied to the goods. Section 22(3). Alternatively, it may be shown that responsibility for a description had been disclaimed, whether by publication of a notice or otherwise. Section See, e.g.; *Norman v. Bennett* (1974) 3 All E.R. 351 at 354.

Finally, the Act confers a special defence against offences committed by the publication of advertisements. Section 22 (4). This defence - of particular relevance to the proprietors of newspapers and magazines - is made out by a defendant who shows that he is a person whose business it is to publish or arrange for the publication of advertisements, and that he received the advertisement for publication in the ordinary course of business and did not know and had no reason to suspect that its publication would amount to an offence referred to in the Act.

PENALTIES

The Act provides a comprehensive and flexible range of penalties. Section 17. A conviction will lead to a fine, a term of imprisonment or to a combination of both. A court, in determining sentence, may take into consideration any corrective advertising carried out by or on behalf of the person charged.

The maximum fine possible on summary conviction is £500, and on conviction on indictment is £10,000. Imprisonment can be imposed for a term not exceeding six months in summary proceedings, and for a term not exceeding two years in proceedings on indictment. In reality, one would expect the sanction of imprisonment to be used only in rare and extreme cases.

An additional penalty of forfeiture - whereby offending goods may be removed from circulation - although not expressly referred to in the Act, is still permissible under the earlier Merchandise Marks legislation.

The discretionary power of a court, to award as compensation all or part of an imposed fine, probably represents the most striking feature of the penalties section. A close reading shows, however, the narrow circumscriptions on this power. It arises only when an offence referred to in the Act has been prosecuted to a *summary* conviction. A person who has suffered loss as a result of the offence must moreover, in order to qualify for compensation, have been called as a prosecution witness in the proceedings. Finally, compensation may not be awarded in a criminal case if a civil action for redress has already commenced.

A contract of goods or services will be rendered neither void nor unenforceable as a result only of a contravention of the Act. Section 25. The express provision on this point pre-empts difficulties of construction under a common law doctrine by which contracts, which are related to an activity prohibited by statute, may as a matter of construction of the statute be adjudged nugatory. See, e.g., *Somers v. Nicholls* (1955) I.R. 83.

SUPERVISION OF THE ACT

The Director of Consumer Affairs

The major responsibility for the overall supervision of the Act lies with the office of the Director of Consumer Affairs. Section 9. That office is an important one; the Director's role as conceived effectively casts him as a consumer's ombudsman.

The establishment terms of the Director's Office ensure a high degree of political independence to its incumbent. The Director is selected by open examination of the Civil Service Commissioners: a candidate need not be a civil servant, although he becomes one if successful. Appointments are for a period - which is renewable - of five years. The Minister may remove a Director at any time, but he must then explain the removal to both Houses of the Oireachtas.

The Director's functions under the Consumer Information Act, 1978, and the Sale of Goods and Supply of Services Act, 1980, divide into several distinct categories. Certain of his functions are of an investigative nature: he must keep advertising practices under general review, and must carry out examinations of such practices if and when the public interest so requires. The Director also has what may be termed functions in persuasion. He can request that misleading practices be discontinued, so that expressions used in such practices be clarified. He has, in addition, a responsibility to encourage and promote codes of standards in relation to advertising.

A further category of functions enable the Director to compel compliance with the Act. He can apply to the High Court for banning orders to enjoin misleading practices, and can also prosecute offences referred to in the Act.

The Act also invests the Director with educational functions - he must ensure, at his discretion, that due publicity be given to legislation which has consumer import.

In addition, the Director is obliged to furnish an annual report to the Minister, and this report is ultimately laid before each House of the Oireachtas.

Finally, the functions of the Director have been increased by Section 55, S.G.S.S.A., 1980, to cover aspects of the supervision of that legislation. Section 55 is as follows:—

"(1) The Director of Consumer Affairs shall have the following additional functions—

(a) to keep under general review practices or proposed practices in relation to any of the obligations imposed on persons by any provision of this Act.

(b). to carry out examinations of any such practices or proposed practices where the Director considers that, in the public interest, such examinations are proper or the Minister so requests.

(c) to request persons engaging in or proposing to engage in such practices as are, or are likely to be, contrary to the obligations imposed on them by any provision of this Act to discontinue or refrain from such practices.

(2) The Minister may by order confer on the Director of Consumer Affairs such further functions as he considers appropriate for the purposes of this Act".

Authorised Officers

Provision is made for an inspectorate to assist in the implementation of the Act. Section 16.

This body comprises authorised officers of either the Minister or local authorities.

The functions of the authorised officers are exclusively investigative. 'The powers conferred to enable the carrying out of these functions equate generally with those of the Revenue Commissioners. First, an authorised officer can at all reasonable times enter and inspect a business premises, and buy goods therein. He can, require the production of records and information relating to the business. Thirdly, he can inspect, copy or take extracts from such records. Fourthly, he can require information regarding any person engaged in the business. An authorised officer can, fifthly, require any other information pertinent to his inquiries.

Because of its extensive powers, the inspectorate is to be composed only of whole-time officers.

TABLE OF CASES

TABLE OF STATUTES

INDEX

APPENDIX

EXTRACTS FROM EUROPEAN COMMUNITIES (UNFAIR TERMS IN CONSUMER CONTRACTS) REGULATIONS, 1995.

3. (1) Subject to the provisions of Schedule 1, these Regulations apply to any term in a contract concluded between a seller of goods or supplier of services and a consumer which has not been individually negotiated.

    (2) For the purpose of these Regulations a contractual term shall be regarded as unfair if, contrary to the requirement of good faith, it causes a significant imbalance in the parties' rights and obligations under the contract to the detriment of the consumer, taking into account the nature of the goods or services for which the contract was concluded and all circumstances attending the conclusion of the contract and all other terms of the contract or of another contract on which it is dependent.

    (3) In determining whether a term satisfies the requirement of good faith, regard shall be had to the matters specified in Schedule 2

to these Regulations.

(4) A term shall always be regarded as having not been individually negotiated where it has been drafted in advance and the consumer has therefore not been able to influence its substance, particularly in the context of a pre-formulated standard contract.

(5) The fact that a specific term or any aspect of a term has been individually negotiated shall not exclude the application of this Regulation to the rest of the contract if an overall assessment of the contract indicates that it is nevertheless a contract as described in paragraph (4) of this Regulation referred to in Article 3.2 of the Council Directive as a pre-formulated standard contract.

(6) It shall be for any seller or supplier who claims that a term was individually negotiated to show that it was.

(7) An indicative and non-exhaustive list of the terms which may be regarded as unfair, pursuant to Article 3.3 of the Council Directive, is set out in the Annex to the Directive and in Schedule 3 to these Regulations.

4.   A term shall not of itself be considered to be unfair by relation to the definition of the main subject matter of the contract or to the adequacy of the price and remuneration, as against the goods and services supplied, in so far as these terms are in plain, intelligible language.

5.   (1) In the case of contracts where all or certain terms offered to the consumer are in writing, the seller or supplier shall ensure that terms are drafted in plain, intelligible language.

   (2) Where there is a doubt about the meaning of a term, the interpretation most favourable to the consumer shall prevail.

6.   (1) An unfair term in a contract concluded with a consumer by a seller or supplier shall not be binding on the consumer.

   (2) The contract shall continue to bind the parties, if it is capable of continuing in existence without the unfair term.

7.   These Regulations shall apply notwithstanding any contract term which applies or purports to apply the law of a country other than a Member State and would

thereby deprive a consumer of protection under the Council Directive.

8. (1) The Director may apply to the High Court for, and may at the discretion of the Court, be granted, an order prohibiting the use or, as may be appropriate, the continued use of any term in contracts concluded by sellers or suppliers adjudged by the Court to be an unfair term.

(2) The Director shall cause to be published notice of intention to apply to the High Court for an order under paragraph (1) of this Regulation in Iris Oifigiúil and at least two national newspapers and in such further or other manner as the Court may direct.

(3) Every person claiming to have an interest in any such application shall be entitled to appear before and be heard by the Court on the hearing of the application.

(4) On any such application it shall not be necessary for the Director or any such person to prove-
     (a)   actual loss or damage, or
     (b)   recklessness or negligence on the part of the seller or supplier.

(5) In the exercise of its jurisdiction under paragraph (1) of this Regulation the Court shall take account of all the interests involved and in particular the public interest.

(6) Paragraph (1) of this Regulation is without prejudice to the right of a consumer to rely on the provisions of these Regulations in any case before a court of competent jurisdiction.

9. In determining whether or not the terms of a contract are unfair account shall be taken of all its features and in particular of any information it contains concerning the matters set out in the Annex to the Council Directive and in Schedule 3 to these Regulations.